TOM BRADY

by K.C. Kelley

Consultant: Craig Ellenport
Former Senior Editor
NFL.com

BEARPORT
PUBLISHING

New York, New York

Credits

Cover, © Geoff Burke/USA Today Sports; 4, © Trog Nguyen/Shutterstock; 4–5, © AP Photo/Eric Gay; 6, Courtesy Junípero Serra High; 7, Courtesy Junípero Serra High School; 8, © AP File Photo/NFL Photos; 8–9, © Joe Robbins; 11, © AP Photo/Michael Dwyer; 12–13, © Jim Bourg/Reuters/Newscom; 14, © Robert E. Klein/Icon SMI 461/Newscom; 14–15, © Tom Briglia 230/Icon SMI/Newscom; 16–17, © AP Photo/David Goldman; 18, © Evan Agostini/Invision/AP; 18–19, © Tribune Content Agency LLC/Newscome; 20, © AP Photo/Patrick Semansky; 20–21, © Kevin Dietsch/UPI/Newsroom; 22, © Cliff Welch/Icon SMI/Newscom; 23, © AP Photo/Eric Gay.

Publisher: Kenn Goin
Senior Editor: Joyce Tavolacci
Creative Director: Spencer Brinker
Production and Photo Research: Shoreline Publishing Group LLC

Library of Congress Cataloging-in-Publication Data

Names: Kelley, K. C., author.
Title: Tom Brady / by K.C. Kelley.
Description: New York, New York : Bearport Publishing Company, Inc., [2018] |
    Series: Amazing Americans: Football Stars | Includes webography. |
    Includes bibliographical references and index.
Identifiers: LCCN 2017040940 (print) | LCCN 2017042434 (ebook) |
    ISBN 9781684025107 (ebook) | ISBN 9781684024520 (Library)
Subjects: LCSH: Brady, Tom, 1977-—Juvenile literature. | Football
    players—United States—Biography—Juvenile literature. | New England
    Patriots (Football team)—History—Juvenile literature.
Classification: LCC GV939.B685 (ebook) | LCC GV939.B685 K45 2018 (print) |
    DDC 796.332092 [B] —dc23
LC record available at https://lccn.loc.gov/2017040940

For more information, write to Bearport Publishing Company, Inc., 45 West 21st Street, Suite 3B, New York, New York 10010. Printed in the United States of America.

10 9 8 7 6 5 4 3 2 1

CONTENTS

Super Bowl Star

Minutes were left in **Super Bowl** LI (51). Tom Brady was in trouble. His team, the New England Patriots, trailed the Atlanta Falcons, 28–3. Tom took charge. He threw one perfect pass after another. The Patriots won the game!

Super Bowl LI (51) was held at NRG Stadium in Houston, Texas.

Tom led the Patriots to the biggest comeback in Super Bowl history!

Young Brady

Tom Brady was born in San Mateo, California, on August 3, 1977. As a child, he loved football, but he was small. His parents worried he might get hurt. Finally, in ninth grade, Tom got to play. He was not big or fast, but he was a leader. In eleventh grade, Tom became **quarterback**!

Tom (center) in high school

In his first high school game, Tom was **sacked** 15 times!

Tom as a high school student

College Man

After high school, Tom went to the University of Michigan. However, the football team already had a quarterback. Tom had to work hard and wait. When he got his chance to play, Tom wowed everyone. He led Michigan to 20 wins in two seasons!

Tom (#10) gets ready to hand off the ball to a teammate.

Tom uses his powerful passing arm to hurl the ball.

As a senior, Tom led the Michigan Wolverines to four exciting comeback wins.

To the NFL

Tom was ready to play with the pros! The New England Patriots picked him for their team. Like Michigan, however, the Patriots already had a **starter**. Tom would have to wait again, but he never lost hope. "I'm the best decision your [team] has ever made," Tom told the owner of the Patriots.

Tom was the 199th player chosen in the 2000 **NFL Draft**.

Tom (right) with Patriots
starter Drew Bledsoe (left)

★ 11

MVP!

In 2001, Tom got his chance to shine when quarterback Drew Bledsoe got hurt. Tom led the team to 11 wins. Then he guided the Patriots to the Super Bowl— and they won!

Tom became the youngest player ever named Super Bowl **MVP.**

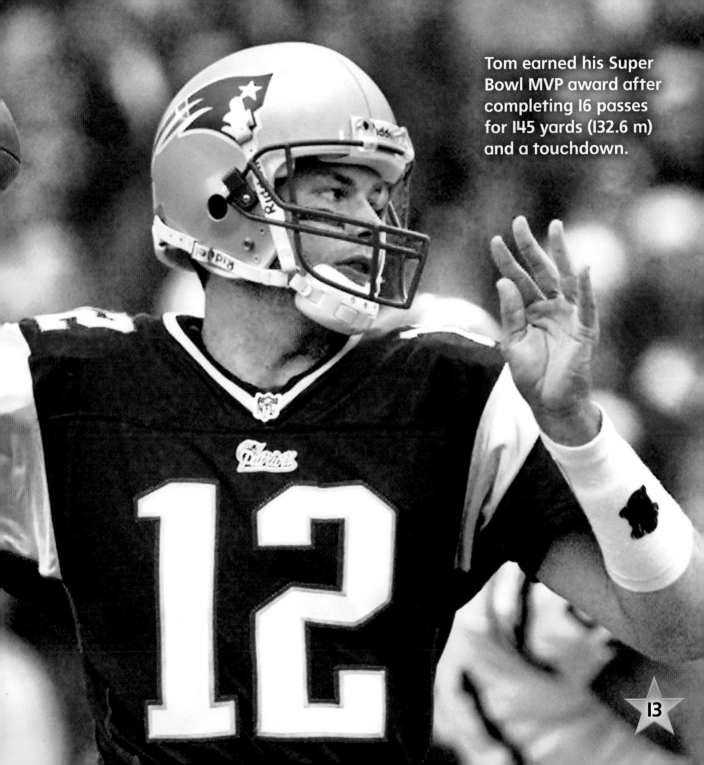

Tom earned his Super Bowl MVP award after completing 16 passes for 145 yards (132.6 m) and a touchdown.

13

Patriots Power

With Tom in charge, the Patriots became the NFL's top team. They won back-to-back Super Bowls. In 2007, Tom set an NFL record with 50 touchdown passes!

Tom was also named NFL MVP in 2007 and 2010.

During the 2007 season, the Patriots had a 16–0 record—thanks to Tom.

A Shocking Win

In 2014, Tom led the Patriots to another Super Bowl. With 15 minutes left, New England trailed the Seattle Seahawks, 24–14. The Patriots needed a big comeback. Tom led the team on two long touchdown drives. The Patriots won the game, 28–24!

In 2014, Tom was named to his tenth Pro Bowl, the NFL's all-star game.

Tom calls out a play to his teammates during Super Bowl XLIX (49).

Ready for More!

How does Tom keep playing his very best? He takes care of his body. Tom works out at the gym every day. He also eats healthy foods. "I want to play until I'm in my mid-40s," he says with a smile.

Tom turned 40 in 2017.

Tom plays with his son John while his wife holds Benjamin.

Tom married model Gisele Bündchen in 2009. He has three children—Vivian, John, and Benjamin.

A Good Son

During the 2016 season, Tom's mom was very sick. Tom said to her, "Don't worry, we are going to make sure you come to [the Super Bowl]." Tom kept his promise. As his mom watched, Tom led the Patriots to another Super Bowl win!

Tom with his wife, daughter, and mom (right) after the Super Bowl

Tom became the first quarterback to win five Super Bowls.

21

Here are some key dates in Tom Brady's life.

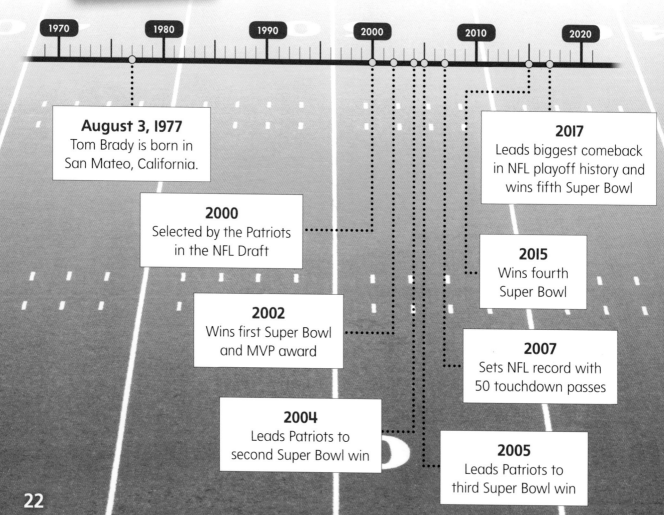

| 1970 | 1980 | 1990 | 2000 | 2010 | 2020 |

August 3, 1977
Tom Brady is born in San Mateo, California.

2000
Selected by the Patriots in the NFL Draft

2002
Wins first Super Bowl and MVP award

2004
Leads Patriots to second Super Bowl win

2017
Leads biggest comeback in NFL playoff history and wins fifth Super Bowl

2015
Wins fourth Super Bowl

2007
Sets NFL record with 50 touchdown passes

2005
Leads Patriots to third Super Bowl win

Glossary

MVP (EM-VEE-PEE) letters standing for the most valuable player, an award given to the best player in a game or in a season

NFL Draft (EN-EFF-ELL DRAFT) an annual event in which NFL teams choose college players to join their teams

quarterback (KWOR-tur-bak) a football player who leads the offense, the part of a team that moves the ball forward

sacked (SAKD) when a quarterback is tackled while he is trying to pass the ball

starter (STAR-tur) the coach's first choice to play in a game

Super Bowl (SOO-pur BOHL) the NFL's championship game

Index

Read More

Allen, Kathy. *Tom Brady
(Football Stars Up Close).*
New York: Bearport (2014).

Braun, Eric. *Tom Brady
(Sports All-Stars).* Minneapolis,
MN: Lerner (2017).

Learn More Online

To learn more about Tom Brady, visit
www.bearportpublishing.com/AmazingAmericans

About the Author

K.C. Kelley has written more than 100 books for
young readers, including many about sports.

This handbook belongs to:

_____

_____

_____

For Nancy and Janet

First edition 2015

Library of Congress Catalog Card Number 2014953086
ISBN 978-0-7636-7417-5

15 16 17 18 19 20 CCP 10 9 8 7 6 5 4 3 2 1
Printed in Shenzhen, Guangdong, China

This book was typeset in Joe.
The illustrations were done in acrylic.

Candlewick Press
99 Dover Street
Somerville, Massachusetts 02144

visit us at www.candlewick.com

Ragweed's Farm Dog Handbook

Anne Vittur Kennedy

CANDLEWICK PRESS

I'm Ragweed. I'm a farm dog,
and I'm really, really good at it.
Most dogs aren't.

But don't worry. You'll be great.
You have the handbook.

Here's the first thing you need to know:
The rooster wakes the farmer early in the morning.

That's his job. That's not your job.
Don't wake the farmer.
You will really, really want to wake the farmer.
But don't wake the farmer.

If you DO wake the farmer,

you can get a biscuit
just to go away.

Next, you need to know about pigs.
Pigs lie in the mud all day and get bigger and BIGGER.
That's their job. That's not your job.
Don't lie in the mud.

Mud is lovely.
It smells like worms and toes and earwax,
so you will really, really want to lie in the mud.
But don't lie in the mud.

If you DO lie in the mud, you will get a bath,
which is not lovely at all.

But you will get a biscuit after the bath.
So, OK then.

Now, about chickens.
Chickens sit on their nests and lay eggs.
That's their job. That's not your job.
Don't sit on their nests.

You will really, really want
to sit on their nests.
But don't sit on their nests.

If you DO sit on their nests,

Bonus advice:
Pretend you were chasing
a fox away and you will get
THREE biscuits!

(Give the fox one.)

Sheep grow curly hair,

which is used to make yarn

to knit sweaters for city dogs.

Sheep are fun to chase, too.
But that's not your job. Don't chase the sheep.

You will really, really want to chase the sheep.
But don't chase the sheep.

Exception:
If the farmer is away, chase the sheep!

Cows eat grass all day and make milk.

That's their job. That's not your job.
Don't eat grass.

You will really, really want to eat grass.
But don't eat grass.

If you DO eat grass, you won't get a biscuit.

But you will throw up a biscuit,
and you can eat that one again.

So, that's how to be a good farm dog.
Let's review what you've learned:

The rooster wakes the farmer.

Pigs get bigger and bigger.

Chickens lay eggs.

Sheep grow curly hair.

Cows make milk.

And what's the farm dog's job?

TO GET BISCUITS!

Now here's the best part. Watch this.
This is when I sit on the porch with the farmer.
He pats my head and tells me I'm a good farm dog.

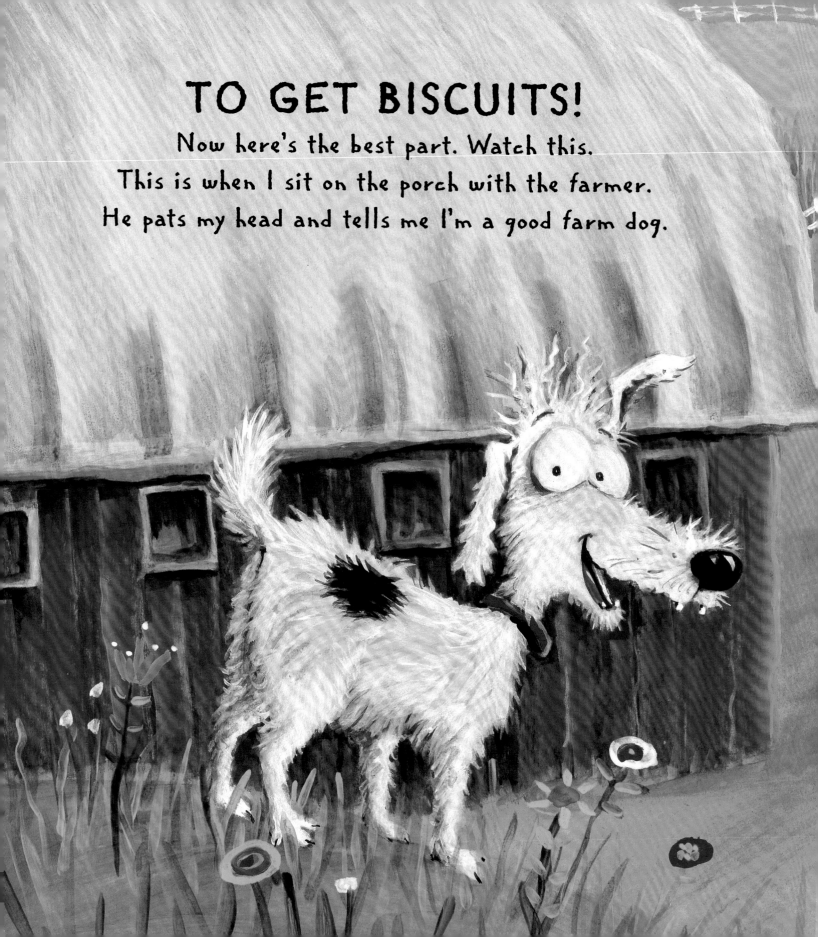

Then I get a biscuit. Just for that!

You're going to love this job.